The Poetry of Teaching

Poets were the first teachers of mankind
...Horace

Hermon Card

Thornetree Hill Poetry Press

The Poetry of Teaching
Copyright © 1998 by Hermon R. Card

ISBN 0-9664103-2-7

For information, contact
Thornetree Hill Poetry Press
P.O. Box 15088, Syracuse, NY 13215

To Dee, who turned on the light,
And Nick, who showed me the way.

In my life as a teacher, I have learned more than I have taught and gained more than I have given. Teaching has made me a better person, a more complete person. I am truly grateful to the two thousand-plus students who inspired me, not only to write this poetry, but to live it.

Contents

Poets were the first teachers of mankind

...Horace

Resurrection

Teaching is about
Recreating ourselves
    Changing
    Evolving

Surrendering annually
    To the heat
    Of late June
Burning ourselves to ash
    The residue
    Of our own intensity
    Our own energy
Consumed by our own fire

And in September
    Rising
    Phoenix-like
With new life
    New energy
To fly on strong
    New wings

First Day on the Job

"I had no training for this job." I thought to myself,
so how did I get here?
What kind of joke is this
that I'm trying to pull on myself?

As soon as these eighth graders figure out
that I don't know diddley squat about it
they are going to take over the room
and If I'm LUCKY only hold me for ransom
and HOPE the school has some kind of policy about
paying off and setting me free.

I suppose if I make enough noise
and appear a bit deranged
it may keep them at bay for awhile.

As long as they think I'm dangerous
I have a chance to survive.
English teachers are supposed to be eccentric
so I'll play that up—do a few things they don't expect,
keep them off stride—
YEAH!! that's the ticket.
Of course, I'll have to come up
with something new tomorrow...

Good Advice

It's really important
that I not figure that
I'm the intellectual giant in the room
because
when I do,
the odds are pretty good
that someone
is going to prove me
wrong.

Guru

I've always wanted to be a guru,
my disciples gathered around me
entreating me to provide them
with some great truth
some key to their existence,
a word which would propel them to greatness.
"Master, what is the meaning of life?"
for example.

My students on the other hand
seem to seek lesser truths,
keys to somewhat less loftier ambition
yet, desiring the answers to questions
as seemingly unanswerable
as the meaning of life.

"How long should it be?"
"Does spelling count?"

It's neither that I can't answer those questions
nor that I don't want to
but they hardly seem worthy of a guru.

on the other hand,
I don't KNOW the meaning of life
and if I did I sure wouldn't be here
teaching English and I
don't think I would get much of a kick out
sitting in a lotus position all day
dispensing esoteric advice anyway.

Let's just leave it that the piece should be l
long enough to get the job done,
and of course spelling counts.

Attitudes

I have to be careful
not to let the things
in my job which irritate me
turn me against my work.

For every bad student I have many good ones
For every rudeness there are many kindnesses
For every failure there are many successes
For all the shoddiness there is artistry

for every outburst of anger
there are peals of laughter
For every downcast eye
there are twinkles in another

I will never change
all the bad to good
But I will never let that
turn me against my work.

Many times I start the day
with the attitude that
there are a lot of things wrong
      with my students
      with my job
      with my life

and this is true

But if there were not
the wrong things,
to what would I compare
what is good?

if all was good, then
I would eventually find
something that was
less good than the rest
and complain about it,
but is the bad
which makes the good
stand out.
And I will never let that
turn me against my work.

An Odd Kid

In eighth grade Johnny liked to talk about plants—
what he grew and why.
A loner, an odd kid.

He was still into it in high school,
growing things—
plants he couldn't even get high on.
Still a loner, an odd kid.

Ten years or so ago I saw him in a market,
just up from Florida
with some race horses he was training.
Sleeping in the horse barn—
a loner, an odd kid.

Two years ago,
dead of AIDS,
he rated a news article, not just an obituary—
public testimony to his life as
a loner, an odd kid.

Teachers recalled him as that.
"Really into plants, flowers and stuff," they said.
"Trained horses," I added.
"Loner, odd kid," they affirmed.

He loved living things
plants, animals, people.
Too bad that's what
we think makes for
a loner, an odd kid.

Keep it Simple

First day of school
for both my granddaughter
and me.

Kate's first,
my twenty-first.

I always make it
something tricky,
the first step of a quest
to make something meaningful
of 125 eighth graders,
a great responsibility,
a magnificent Holy Grail-like search for
some great truth,
some essential knowledge.

She, on the other hand,
made some friends
and had a snack.

Random thoughts about teaching:

Society

Seventh grade boys who
weigh about seventy pounds
fear the girls who are

bigger and stronger,
waiting for the day when they
will be able to

talk without fear of
sounding like an old hinge
and be tall enough

to see
and be seen
in the hall.

Scientific Theory

Is it possible
that I use chalk that is
not in the spectrum

of visible light
and speak in a voice that can't
be heard by students?

Autobiography

She didn't really want
to write her autobiography—
only the part that

She really didn't
want to remember but was
all she ever could.

She hasn't got much
to say that anybody
would want to read.

Who cares about what
happened to her when she was six
and seven and eight,

until she and Mom
moved to this town, away
from good old Uncle Bob?

Reflection

Every now and then
I find myself irritated
at a student
for behaving the way that I did
in eighth grade

and I hope that I respond
as well as my teachers did.

End of the Year

As I begin the annual archaeological
dig that is my end of the year clean up
I stare at the remnants
of the school year
trying to decide
the quality of the last ten months,
looking for clues
to tell me if what I had done
had made a difference.

If I was smart
I would just dump everything paper
into the recycling bin
and all the rest
into the trash
and be done with it

But I'm compelled
to examine everything
to determine its relevance
to my teaching.

Do I save it, recycle it, trash it?
(Isn't that the same question
I ask about my students?)

It's tough to consign to the trash
the piece that she labored over
for three weeks,
grimacing
every time I called her to my desk
for a conference
until I finally half-smiled
at its almost-doneness

and told her "one more draft should do it."
Her sigh of relief
scattered papers on my desk
and her smile
scattered my doubts...

Nothing to save from
the paltry output
of one of my brightest students,
stuck in a self-defeating rut,
producing nothing but
heartache for mom,
frustration for me,
tears for himself...

I suppose I should save her poetry
For when she's able
to return for it,
but for now I just
read her cries of pain,
her torment flowing
from line to line
like the tears
down her anorexic cheeks...

How can his poem,
a masterpiece only to him
filled with contrived
references to flatulence
be anything but trash?
Well, it is the best thing
he wrote...

So, for the twentieth or so time
I save everything—maybe not
in a box or folder,
but somewhere
within me, that place where teachers
keep everything that
makes them a bit sad
to leave in June,
and a bit happy
to return in September.

Wm .

William was a pain in the butt.

I tried my best to make allowances for
his father being in jail
his being in a foster home
his being a city kid in a country school and
his having the social skills of a hyena

But it wasn't good enough and when
he got suspended
I was happy and when
he got sent to the alternative Ed. program
I was really happy.

I know there wasn't anything
I could have done to change things

but when the handwritten addendum
to the attendance list read
Wm. Wilson Jr. left as of 10/23/95
I was angry at myself.

14

First Person Singular

At my school
with a minority population of
less than two percent,
diversity has to do with differences
in height
or hair color
or who you hang out with.

To the lone African American
student in my class
I tried to explain
the correctness of

"I am"
versus the incorrectness of

"I be"

I am? You mean like
I am black?
I am different?
I am mocked?
I am bullied?
I am afraid?
I am alone?

Hey—why not just let me **be**?

Small Town Tough Guy

I can't write no poetry
I do OK with songs though
Poetry ain't for guys like me, man
Stuff I do ain't poetry man
It's real stuff you know
drugs and shit like that
Poetry's for dudes with problems
Dudes who need love and pretty stuff
I got what I need
a guitar and a guy who can get me high
'Course I ain't no Jimi Hendrix yet
I mean I don't play too good
and I ain't really done much drugs
But I gotta keep up
Can't let on what I'm really like
It ain't easy bein' a bad dude in this town—too many poets.

Living in Another Land

She sat in the back of the room—
Just across the border that separates
The land of the regular kids
From the uncharted territory she calls home.

It's a beautifully vibrant land—
Rolling, fruitful plains of imagination and creativity,
Vast, deep oceans of talent and potential
Majestic mountains of eccentric, quirky behavior.

It's also a somber land—
A great desert of loneliness,
Uncrossable chasms of isolation,
Manmade barriers of stereotyped expectation.

I didn't visit her often enough—
The border crossing was arduous,
And I would have to leave too much
at the customs house.

The Voice

Listen for the voice.
It will speak loudly,
softly,
urgently,
calmly.

It will be assertive
It will be frightened
It will be proud
It will be plaintive

It will scream
It will beg
it will laugh
It will cry

it will speak in odd places
odd styles
odd words
It will tell you things you need to know
It will tell you things you don't
It will tell you things you want to know
It will tell you things you won't

And when it does,
listen.

$1.78

So I get this letter
from a father whose son is a
product of maternal
indulgence and apologizing
suggesting that maybe I don't know
my ass from a hot rock
about teaching
and wants to know why I'm more interested
in grabbing the big tax dollars he pays
than I am about teaching.
So after I explain that
he came to his conclusion without
being armed with all the facts of the matter
and he turns red
and apologizes several times
and winds up explaining
through teary eyes
what things are like at home
and apologizes a few more times
and tells me to go ahead
and give his son another detention
and he'll be sure it gets served,
I decide I won't embarrass him
by returning the buck seventy-eight
which I figure is his share of my salary
and walk out of the room
feeling lousy
for planning to in the first place.

Mrs. Thomas

Mrs. Thomas was a hard,
demanding,
drill sergeant of
an eighth grade English teacher,

who scared us daily,
tested
us weekly, and
smiled, maybe, monthly.

She read to us, in her
no-nonsense
you'd-better-pay-attention voice,
from "Man without a Country".

At the part where
Philip Nolan
was really wishing he had
kept his mouth shut

the principal walked in
quietly,
whispered in her ear,
and left.

In her no-nonsense way,
Mrs. Thomas,
in her best voice, told us
that Coach Conwicke had died,

then excused herself
politely,
walked out of the room,
and left us alone.

She returned to our
puzzled silence,
wiped away a tear
that had escaped her,

and resumed her
no-nonsense reading,
becoming again the
Mrs. Thomas we knew.

But, not really.

Times Have Changed in Eighth Grade Writing

When I was in eighth grade
in nineteen fifty-nine
I wrote of
baseball
and Christmas
and summer
and family
and fun
and other stuff that eighth graders knew

My students in eighth grade
in nineteen ninety-six
write of
hunger
and poverty
and crime
and divorce
and abortion
and abuse
and other stuff that eight graders know.

1986—When I Got Good at It

Ten years of teaching
adjectives and verbs
and to not write run on sentences

had not really made me
any kind of teacher
but had made me

the guy who had to explain
to the bored eyes
and empty faces

why we had to do this
and what the point was
and all that stuff.

Then I spent some time
reading seniors' autobiographies
in a class I had invented

(when the department chairman said
"Hey, we gotta use these books so use 'em.")
and I read about
first love
and lost love
and moving
and changing
and growing
and longing
and laughing
and hurting

and I read things
which amused me
and confused me
and sobered me
and bored me
and delighted me
and scared me
and angered me

and I read about
her Mom's suicide
and his dog dying
and his alcoholic mother
and her parents' divorce
and his Dad's death in Viet Nam
and her little sister's leukemia

and I knew that there was more to this than
ten years of teaching
adjectives and verbs
and to not write run on sentences.

Beyond the Classroom

We must look beyond the classroom,
to see what's really there
We must reach beyond the classroom,
to really be aware

We must act beyond the classroom,
and model with our deeds.
We must care beyond the classroom,
to know our students' needs

We must think beyond the classroom,
and to their minds appeal,
We must teach beyond the classroom,
to make it all seem real

We must dream beyond the classroom,
to help extend their reach,
We must move beyond the classroom,
if we're to truly teach.

To Some Retiring Friends

Years pass, unnoticed, uncounted
Students too—hundreds, thousands,
many now nameless, faceless
to you, but not the other way.

You may not know them now,
but they know you.
You took them somewhere
unreachable without you.

You gave them
what they needed,
(perhaps more).

They remember
what you've done,

counseled,
disciplined,
tested,
prodded,
coached,
encouraged.

We remember
what you've done,

Given of yourselves—
for them,
for us.

Room Full of Poets

So, when I ask who in the class is a poet
I get maybe three or four hands
raised and maybe a couple more after some
shifty-eyed glances
to see who else's hand went up
and to figure if it was cool to raise their own.

So then I tell them that everybody's a poet and
most of the non-raisers don't believe me
(and I even question my own veracity a bit)
I ask them how come they think
they're NOT poets
and roll my eyes at them
when I get the "I can't rhyme" response
and tell them that we poets
voted to revoke that law and that
anybody with feelings is a poet
and they have feelings
so they must be poets.

"Oh sure." They think,
and they say "yeah, but
we can't write them down
so good
'cause we don't think like poets
and we don't talk like poets
and we   sur r r r r r r e don't write like poets."

And I ask them what that's all about,
that talking and thinking and writing business.
Who made those rules?

Who said how you
have to think and talk and write?
Isn't it enough to just do it?

Naa---It's gotta sound fancy and smart and
'Englishy' they say
and sound like a greeting card when you read it
and...you know...

Maybe I know and maybe I don't
I say
but I do know this:
The poetry is not in the language.
The poetry is in you.

Teaching Poetry

There is intense pressure
on one who would teach
the writing of poetry,
for he
or she
might create
poets,
and the accompanying responsibility
is immense,
for poets are powerful people
who hold in their hands
Emotions,
Theirs,
ours,
and these poets,
throughout history,
have been revered for
their ability to bring
the word
from the *Otherworld* as the Celts called it
and
the word,
reaches inside,
takes control
and brings pain
and joy
and confusion
and ecstasy
and satisfies our longing
for the answer to questions
of love
and beauty

and the mysteries
which confound us
eternally.
So if you would create
these poets
you must bear the responsibility
for their actions
and the effect they
have on themselves
and on us
and on the universe.

Signs of Success

I have done my job
when the fist-pumping "Yeah!"
is the result of
a decent haiku.

And the extended
"cooowullll"
sneaks out of a writing group

and poetry books show up
on the library's overdue list.

Success—1998

They are told that success
takes the form of a high grade
a gold star or a smiling face affixed to
a piece of work they
have labored over
or copied
or downloaded from the Internet

The substance of the grade for them
is simply its form
and the status it conveys
in the "wha'd ya gets?"

What better way to confuse them
than to give grades based
on the quality of the piece rather
than the quality of the font used
when they typed it on the Mac
or the graphics
from www.goodgrades.com

The Poetry of Teaching

I have been employed as a teacher
for twenty-three years.
I've been a good one
for about twelve.

Before you suggest I write a poem
as tribute to tenure,
let me explain—
As hard as we try,
we can't be taught to teach.
We can be taught how,
but the rest is up to us.
After awhile, I figured out how.

The time I became
pretty good at teaching
was about the time
I returned
to writing poetry.
I hadn't written a poem
for years
not because
I had nothing to write,
but because I had no sense of
what it was
I had to say.

The words were there,
but what was behind them?
I was good with words,
but not with feelings.

In writing poetry
we become honest
 poetry can only come
from honesty,
because it can only come from within us.
If we cannot be honest
about our feelings,
we can't write.
If we cannot be honest with ourselves
we can't teach,
because we can't care about others.
Teaching, and poetry,
involve sharing and revealing ourselves,
exposing what is inside us
to others,
so that they can take advantage
of what we have to offer.

The Heart of Teaching

The heart of teaching
beats in us—
rapidly as we excel,
slowly as we falter,
but strong, always strong.
Fueled by courage
and will
and the desire
to make better the lives
of those who need us,
trust us,
sometimes admire us,
and often,
frustrate us.

The heart of teaching
beats steadily—
renewing us
keeping us
alive with
the energy
to teach
to learn
to make better the lives
of those who need us,
trust us,
sometimes admire us,
and often
frustrate us.

The heart of teaching
beats
in
us.

Her Way

She came to my desk
and told me that
she could write it my way
and it would be shit
but,
if she did it her way
it would be good.

It never occurred to me
that I didn't much like students
using the word "shit" in my classroom

and opted for the latter.
And it was personal
and clever
and deep
and wistful
and exotic
and painful
and happy
and tragic
and funny

and it was all these things
because it was her life

and,
if she did it her way
it would be good.

The Work of Teaching

Teaching is hard work,
demanding work,
unfinished work.

It is not work which fills me with
the acid-sharp eye-burning pulp mill
air of Bogalusa
or the white-hot lung-searing auto plant
air of Detroit
or the razor-cold blood-freezing ship yard
air of Duluth
It doesn't lower me into the
deadly dust and body breaking
labor of the coal mines
of my great great grandfather in Wales
or his son in West Virginia.
I don't fear the limb devouring saw teeth
of my grandfather's mill
or the ulcerating tension
of my father's law practice.

I do not share
my wife's daily view
of the shattered lives of children.

I do not wallow
in a miserable existence
born of hourly wages feeding too many mouths
nor labor in assembly-line tedium
my intellect
collecting
in a puddle at my feet.

I do not pray for the weekend's brief relief.
I pray instead
for the strength to be patient
and the strength to be kind
and the strength to set an example
in a world where the example is often born of things that I DO
fear—
ignorance
and conceit
and prejudice
and hatred
and abuse.

Teaching is not work born of fame
there is no aspiration to glory
no lavish movie star sidewalk recognition
no numbers retired
no laurels bestowed by Caesar

Teaching is bearing the weight
of the world's children—
too heavy for most—
but not for you, not for me

Teaching is facing the demands of society
to cure its ills
to right its wrongs
to solve what it cannot solve
while it takes the day off

the hardest part, knowing
that the job never gets done.

Students do not roll out of
the pulp mill in Bogalusa or
the auto plant in Detroit or
the ship yard in Duluth

Students roll out of my classroom
and your classroom.
They roll out of every classroom
in every city in the world
and out of every classroom they roll
unfinished and incomplete
because we are unable to put on the final
coat of paint
and buff them to the sheen
we would have them carry for life
because they have built-in flaws
and they have been imperfectly smelted
and baked and refined and cured
and they are prone to rust and decay
and they have weaknesses below the surface
and they have been put together shoddily sometimes
and they have been whisked past the inspectors
too rapidly
and given the final stamp of approval
that simply means
they have been moved
down the conveyor belt
to make room for more raw material.

In the acid-sharp, eye-burning air of Bogalusa ,
the pulp mill turns out a finished product.
In the white-hot, lung-searing air of Detroit,
the auto plant turns out a finished product.
In the razor-cold, blood-freezing air of Duluth,
 the ship yard turns out a finished product.

But the product we turn out
flawed
and imperfect
poorly refined
perhaps
rough in texture
weak below the surface
is the most valuable product turned out anywhere
and it
has a beauty
and a texture
and a gentleness
and a humanity that we give it

even though
teaching is hard work,
demanding work,
unfinished work.

Girl in the Middle

In the middle of the laughing
children was a little girl
wiping tears from her eyes—
not tears of happiness,
but sad, heavy tears

I wanted her to laugh
like the others
I didn't want her
to have pain
that drowned out the happiness
keeping her from sharing
her friends' delight

Maybe they weren't her friends
maybe she had no friends
maybe she had a friend
that was a friend no more

Maybe the poems about
parents and
brothers and
sisters and
dogs
reminded her of something lost.

I wish I hadn't made her cry.
I wish I had been wrong
when I told the class that poems
sometimes make you sad.

That's not what I meant to do.
But maybe that's what
was meant to be.

To My Teacher

Sometimes I am lost
Take my hand—lead me...

Help me understand
what you are teaching

I know it is more than
it seems—more than
just the definition of
plot or what makes irony

I know it is important
or you would not know it.
You would not teach it
You would not want so
much for it to
be part of me.

But I am lost sometimes.
What makes things important?
What makes them worth knowing
Why am I worth teaching it to?
What will I do with it?
What makes me worth your time,
your effort
your pain?
Am I that special to you?

Sometimes I am lost
Take my hand—lead me...

Mind Rivers

There is a certain ease
among newborns,
an ease which must arise from
knowing there is currently
very little
expected of them and
much
to be given them.
Their responsibility is minimal.
Accepting love
and praise
and food
is not a burden.
Being warm and comfortable
in a new place
is not so terribly difficult,
their future not yet a concern

That concern lies elsewhere,
in the world of those
who hold the fortune of
newborns in their hands
and hearts,
who hold the future itself—
who think not
the simple thoughts
of the new mind
but the tangled thoughts
of the old mind,

At what point then,
do minds become old?
What is it that changes the course
of mind-rivers,
directs them over rocks
and boulders
and churns them into
white froth
and whirlpools
and angry waves
dashing against all
that would guide their progress.

Where are old minds born?
How are new minds,
young minds,
changed to old?

What ages them,
changes them
transports them to
places of anger and greed?

When I stand among new minds
am I also among old ones?

I would be among
new minds
but often feel the aging
that is already taking place.
Deep in the eyes is an oldness,
a too-early weathering
and wrinkling
and eroding of spirit

too focused on that
far less important
than survival.

These newborns look to each other and see what?
In the future when they again
look to each other
they will see what?

This early society of theirs—
a day or two together—
longer than they will spend
with most people they will ever meet—
What meaning will they take from it?

They will never again share the bond
they share at this minute,
this hour of new arrival—
they will never again be as equal,

for each has already started on a
path which will diverge
in minutes or hours
from the other
and they will never again
be of new mind.

From this moment
they will be rivers
flowing over uncertain courses
with rough water
and rocky shoals.

It is us,
the parent,
the teacher,
who must be boundaries—
the strong banks,
the guiding levees,
which will enable them
to cut a true
deep channel
through life's tough crust,
as from this moment
they flow
through the future
to the past.

Idle Hands

He spent the better part of an hour
filling in the white spaces
on the cover of his composition book.
No wonder there was
nothing left to write the poem.

The Crime of Rhyme

A problem which oft plagues a student
even the most wise and prudent:

Whenever the chance to write a verse
The problem, and there's nothing worse

arises nearly every time:
the need to make each end line rhyme.

So all the lines you rearrange
they rhyme, but some are mighty strange

and then hurrah! You finally write
the line you've struggled for all night

but then you hit the poets wall
and you can't go on at all

because you need to rhyme with "orange"
and....

Between the Lines

All that prevents him from
devoting his total attention
to the baseball game
is the pile of student writing
between him and the TV,
a stack of cliches and
tired metaphors
worn out by a thousand previous users
and abusers
of the language.

He sifts through the pile
looking for one which will
motivate him to continue on
to a second and a third,
and so forth,
a metaphorical rounding of the bases,
until he has reduced the pile to nothing,
and able to turn his full attention to
the Yankees and Red Sox.

Glancing above his glasses to catch the replay
of Cecil Fielder rocking a line drive
off the green monster
and only getting a single
he ponders the mysterious twist of baseball fate
that penalizes a player for hitting the ball
too hard
like he is penalizing himself for caring
too much
about grading these papers.

So he pores over them
with the Fenway crowd noise
as background
until he chances across a phrase
which makes him grab the remote
and click the ball game into darkness
and stare at the screen
to see the image which has leapt off
the page in front of him
far more vivid than the night-game-green
of Fenway's infield,
reverberating louder than
the crack of Cecil's bat.

Nobody Told Me

In teacher school,
they failed to tell me
about certain things I would need to know,
like hugging the mother of a student,
a mother , a stranger, who clung to me
near his casket,
with grief's old-friend-tightness,
and whispered in my ear
what a good boy he was,
and how proud they were of him,
and how they hoped
he would have been in my class next year,
and that I would have enjoyed
having him as a student.

And they didn't tell me about
looking into the eyes of students
who were his friends and
seeing the confusion,
and the pain they felt
at a turn of events that didn't fit
how they thought life
should be.

They didn't tell me about the eeriness
of a Monday,
and of a hallway
where one less student would walk,
and the void created
by the passing
of one that I didn't know,
feeling the loss,
unable to define it.

In From The Rain

I. Quoting Studs Terkel paraphrasing from the book Aiken-field by Ronald Blythe:

A young town boy,
a working boy,
can come into a place by accident,
maybe an art gallery,
just to get out of the rain
and as he watches that stuff
he becomes a different person.

II.

So I came in from the rain
in 1975
and my art gallery was in a
1930's brick building
and on display were
about 800 works in progress,
art of a sort I wasn't familiar with
and at that moment I began this poem
this life work
of my work of life
although I didn't actually get it on paper
for twenty-one years.

III.

In that building,
my temporary shelter,
I became known for my ability to keep order.
I was hired to do that—to keep order—
and the opinions were expressed:
> *Mr. Card keeps good order,*
> the principal was heard to say
> *Yes sir, he keeps good order,*
> the vice principal was heard to say
> *He's a mean son of a bitch,*
> some students were heard to say.

So keeping order became my forte
and the cafeteria ladies
loved it when I was on duty.
> *He keeps this place in order,*
> they were often heard to say.

And the administrators
loved the way I kept order so much
that they started inventing ways
for me to do just that.
Disorder was discouraged
in this place
and order proudly displayed
for all to see.
The gallery became a monument to order.

And when I asked about the possibilities
of actually TEACHING something,
there were certain individuals
individuals who prized order above all else
who said:

Well, he's really good at keeping order
God knows he's good at it,
but teaching?
Well I don't know,
who would keep order for us?

And I began thinking that myself,
I mean, all these people here
all these teachers who went to school for this,
who have degrees in teaching
graduate degrees
PhDs for Christ's sake!
These are teachers,
not to be bothered with just keeping order.
Me?   College degree in English all right,
Graduate school? US Army Infantry School,
Fort Benning Georgia,
Infantry Company Commander,
a commissioned order keeper.

I tried to take a course in teaching reading
a graduate course to get me on the right track
but my job at the time
Recruiting Officer,
New York Army National Guard
made my professor really nervous.
She told me I probably couldn't handle the class
—I mean look at my background—
college baseball coach,
security policeman,
infantry company commander—
what does this all have to do
with intellect and teaching?

I'm sure she would have
thought differently
if the class room
suddenly came under fire
and I rose to the challenge with some serious
keeping of order,
but I gave in.
I really wasn't that interested in teaching.
I really didn't want to teach,
or so she led me to believe

What I wanted was to live easily and freely
and have money to pay the occasional bill
and travel
and own cool clothes
and drive a decent car
without being obligated to my father.

Work was not a prime ambition.
Two goes at law school
had only showed me that
I didn't want to be a lawyer
though the money would have been OK
and it had been the perfect career
for my father.

There was a nagging thought,
deep in the back of my mind,
that I should stay here.

It was warm
it was dry
it was safe.

I was afraid to leave.

IV.

In 1976 or '77 I became
disenchanted with my role as
order keeper.
There was order around me but
none within
My education—
leading toward teacher certification—
was progressing well,
and eventually,
my inquiries into teaching
coincided with the creation
of a math lab in our school.

The school people knew
nothing of math labs,
and I,
nothing of math,
but it was only a place for remediation
and a place where order must be kept,
although two students at a time
hardly requires the talent
of a master order keeper such as I.

In my duty,
which turned out to be
mostly
about keeping order and
little
about teaching,
I continued to receive praise.

The vice principal commented
that it was a most orderly math lab—
the most orderly he had every seen
and he was equally impressed
with the four color map
of the battle of Gettysburg—
all three days,
plus some of the cavalry action—
that I had drawn on the blackboard.

I invented ways to occupy
the remedial students.
at the remediation machines
the school bought.
Little to do with math
much to do with keeping order.

The highlight of my time there
was meeting my wife.
[I thought she was beautiful
she thought I was rude.
She's still beautiful
and I've improved a bit.]

In the meantime,
I was trying to get myself certified
because an English teacher
was going to take a leave of absence
for eighteen months
and I could really use the cash.
Let's keep in mind that order keeping
and remediating
did not command the big money
and sixty-five bucks a week
didn't go very far.

V.

My attempt to become
certified as a teacher
had run afoul of bureaucracy.

I signed up for student teaching
through my graduate program.
A few days before starting,
the Dean of the School of Education
called to say that I didn't qualify
to student teach
because I was OFFICIALLY enrolled
in the school of higher education administration
not the school of education,
and they weren't in the habit
of handing out student teaching assignments
to just anybody
who wanted to be a teacher
and they would not allow me
to be an exception
simply because
of all things
I wanted to be a teacher.

VI.

My skill as an order keeper paid off.
The superintendent,
and the principal
and the vice principal
realizing that it was
particularly difficult
for a teacher to take over a class in mid-year,
and being concerned about the disorder
this could create

became rapidly sympathetic to my plight
and the superintendent
wrote a letter to the powers that were
which allowed me to count my math lab time,
those six periods a day
of two-at-a-time remediating,
as "a teaching experience in lieu of student teaching"
and pave my way to eighteen months of keeping order
until the first team teacher returned.

What none of us fully understood was
that I knew nothing of teaching English,
but they were satisfied
that order would be kept,
I was satisfied that I would be employed
for a year and a half.

VII.

Once I found myself in a classroom
things changed, though not really a lot.
I was well supplied with
tons of materials
and lesson plans
from my predecessor
It was clear that she didn't want me
screwing up her good work
of the first half of the year
and I'm sure she was suspicious
as to how well qualified
a guy who was a teacher aide
yesterday
could be an English teacher
today.

Not that I didn't share her concern—
I mean it's one thing
to be the guy in charge
another thing entirely
to be the guy in charge.

Fortunately she had been
a pretty good
keeper of order herself
a bit on the parochial side,
but the students were fully prepared
to follow the established routine,
and as long as I was too,
things were likely to proceed
fairly smoothly.
And things did roll along
fairly well.

Occasionally an administrator
observed my class—
probably, I thought,
to insure order was being kept,
and was suitably impressed at
how well I had adapted
to my new surroundings.
and how orderly things were continuing to be.
     You know how eighth graders can be
     they said with a wink.
I chuckled knowingly
which
they of course
took as conspiratorial acceptance
of their conspiracy of order keeping

Oddly enough the students thought I was
teaching because they were used to what
I was doing and thought that it was teaching.
So they memorized like crazy—
prepositions
vocabulary lists
spelling words
and the year passed
in an orderly manner.

VIII.

Suddenly I was in September of a new year
materials in order, folders ready, lists sorted
the entire year's schedule on the blackboard
order ready to be kept.
The vice principal was mighty impressed.
The year passed,
orderly,
quietly
no waves made,
nothing intellectual
irrationally exchanged.
The administrators were thrilled.
The eighteen months
had passed without incident.
I had held the line for the first team.

Then, she threw a monkey wrench into the plan.
She liked it where
she was.
She quit.

IX.

So, here I was, on the first team
a certified teacher ready to move into
high gear.
but on cruise control.

And so, by default though it was
I felt that this would do nicely
until things cleared up outside
and I could get on
to where I really belonged

I managed to burrow into the curriculum
the well laid out
and well ordered
curriculum
which allowed me to invest
not an awful lot of myself in
what I was doing
and to coast along
surviving quite handily
several close calls with staffing reductions
climbing a rope that was burning below me
always the lowest in seniority
but still on the payroll.

Every time I was likely to get the ax,
someone would retire
or be fired
or have a baby.
Blind luck it seemed—
there were probably lots of better teachers
outside in the storm,
and I was still warm and safe.

X.

Now please don't think I was not a good teacher.
I was a very good teacher
particularly if you define teaching as the
ability to transmit information
in such a manner that it is
retained by the students.
My great talent as an order keeper
made me particularly adept at this.
But,
there needed to be something more.

XI.

For some reason, perhaps boredom,
I began to read what my students were writing.
Not that I had been ignoring them
(How else would I be able to assign grades?)
but not in this way.

I began to listen as I read
to hear their voices
to associate the words with the people
to realize that these were people
young, immature, lazy perhaps,
but people, nonetheless.
People who were affected
by life
just as I was
and who suffered
their own defeats
their own tragedies
their own pain
and were expressing it to me.

and expected,
no, more than that,
needed
me to listen
to hear
what they had to say.

And I began to understand
that I had been looking at
the art
all wrong.
I began to see
what was in front of me.

I was no longer a mere guard,
someone hired to watch over the art work,
to merely protect it from wear and tear
dust it off occasionally
watching displays and exhibits come and go.
I had become more of a curator
an appreciator of the works
not only on the surface
but understanding of its content
its meaning, its substance, its depth—
its passion,
understanding just why it was art,
with a responsibility for its future,
its destiny,
charged with the actual care of the art work,
but in turn
caring about it.

I began to realize that
my shelter
was no longer merely
temporary sanctuary from the storm,
but a place where I belonged
a place, indeed where I was
warm and safe.

But that's only symbolic
that's only the poetic part

What I was,
staring out into the sunlight,
was a teacher.

XII.

A young town boy,
a working boy,
can come into a place by accident,
maybe an art gallery,
just to get out of the rain
and as he watches that stuff
he becomes a different person.

What It's All About

"How'd I get here?"
I ask myself a lot
when I'm thinking about
things I could have done
with my life.

If I could have hit a curve,
for example,
and been a little taller,
and a step faster
I could have been playin' ball on TV
and making the big money.

Or if I had hung in there
with law school
I could have been a judge by now
or a senator,
or at least a partner in a firm
and making the big money.

But instead I walked
into a school when I needed a job
and after I caught on
I could have been a principal,
or maybe even a superintendent
and making the big money.

But I'm in a classroom
with a hundred and twenty kids
passing through every day,
trying to give them something that's
not about making the big money.

It's about when a conversation begins
"I had this teacher once...